baby-gami

BABY WRAPPING FOR BEGINNERS

Andrea Sarvady

FOREWORD BY Fern Drillings, RN, MSN

PHOTOGRAPHY BY BILL MILNE | ILLUSTRATIONS BY JOHN STISLOW

CHRONICLE BOOKS

SAN FRANCISCO

Thank you to Jim Grace for the inspiration.

🆀🅿 A QUIRK PACKAGING BOOK
Text copyright © 2005 by Andrea Sarvady.
Photography copyright © 2005 by Bill Milne.
Illustrations copyright © 2005 by John Stislow.

Library of Congress Cataloging-in-Publication Data available.

ISBN-13 : 978-0-8118-4764-3

Manufactured in China

Designed by Lynne Yeamans
Styled by Janet Prusa
Cover design by Jay Peter Salvas

10 9 8 7 6

Chronicle Books LLC
680 Second Street
San Francisco, California 94107

www.chroniclebooks.com

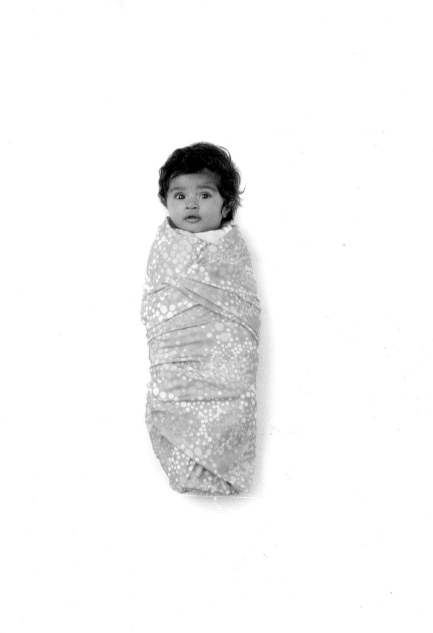

contents

part one: baby wrapping

BASIC WRAPS

EMERGENCY WRAPS

part two: baby wearing

foreword

Swaddling and baby wearing are traditions that go back so far in time that we can't really say when they started. Depictions of babies in "swaddling cloths" have been found in cultures ranging from ancient Greece to the Aztecs to old Japan, and slings of various kinds are found in cultures around the world from Africa to the Arctic. In North America, swaddling has long been practiced in maternity wards, but has only recently begun to gain popularity among parents once they take baby home.

Newborns usually respond very well to being swaddled, perhaps because the feeling resembles how they felt in the womb—warm, cozy, tightly packed—and safe! (When they're free, newborns especially tend to flail their limbs, startling themselves into wakefulness.) They also tend to like being tucked into a sling and worn on mom's or dad's front, perhaps again because it re-creates the feeling of being snug and warm, with a familiar, steady heartbeat providing the background music. Of course, since infants cannot tell us precisely what they like about being swaddled, these are theories developed from observing babies for many years.

Science does have a bit to say on the matter. Several studies have shown that swaddled babies sleep better and longer. It's also been proven that properly wrapped babies have no breathing restrictions, do not overheat, and as long they are not swaddled for hours at a time, do not suffer from hip development problems. These studies confirm what anyone who has spent a lot of time with babies already knows: swaddling a fussy infant will usually quiet and soothe baby, and often send him to sleep.

That is why nurses in maternity wards deliver tightly wrapped, happily snoozing bundles to new parents—who then unwrap them and often can't get them to calm down again until the nurse comes back to re-swaddle!

For all those new parents who wish they could take home a nurse along with their new baby, use this book instead! With humor and patience (two qualities all parents need), *Baby-gami* provides step-by-step instructions, illustrations, and photographs that show exactly how to swaddle a baby into happy comfort— and how to wear a baby for maximum infant delight and parental convenience.

As a childbirth educator and nurse for more than 25 years, I have seen first-hand the benefits of a good swaddle: parents who want to give their babies that feeling of comfort and safety will find the information and instructions in this book indispensable.

Enjoy!

Fern Drillings, RN, MSN

introduction

Congratulations! You've given birth to a beautiful baby. Or adopted one. Or defied the odds and actually found one in a cabbage patch. The point is you're now a parent, with a precious little bundle to call your own.

So how do you bundle that bundle? You've heard from countless parents that babies, especially the newest models, love to be wrapped tightly. Even when babies are older, your ever-present panel of experts advises that babies prefer to be right up on your chest, near the heart and close to the food source.

Why do babies want to be wrapped up and held close? Because it reminds them of the womb, their real home, rather than this frightening, freezing, fun house you've pulled them into. Baby can spend that first crucial month wrapped snug as a bug in a rug. Then you can transfer her to an equally cozy sling and take her on the road. Wraps and slings are heaven for babies. The strange thing is, you'll like them too. Once you get the hang of what we call "baby-gami," you'll find that it's fun to wrap your progeny, and oddly enjoyable to cart her around with you like an oversized necklace. Talk about bling!

This brings us to the real beauty of the baby-gami lifestyle: sleep. Studies have shown that wrapped-up babies sleep longer and better than unwrapped ones. Well, at least longer. And what could be better for the perennially exhausted new parent?

So let the other parents toss their infants into overpriced designer cribs that say "gorgeous" to parents and "terrifying Turkish prison" to babies. Watch other mothers push their babies through the world in monster-truck strollers. You'll be cruising blissfully past them with your new Favorite Human Being gratefully cuddled up against your chest, hearing her little contented snorts and sighs. You'll feel like a million bucks, secure in the knowledge that you're giving your baby the closest thing to a womb you can.

THE SCIENCE OF SWADDLING

Why swaddle? Surely as thoughtful new parents you've read all the important works on childcare, including, of course, Gerard, Harris, and Thach's seminal study on swaddling: *Spontaneous Arousals in Supine Infants While Swaddled and Unswaddled During Rapid Eye Movement and Quiet Sleep.*

In it, the good doctors give thorough research to back up a heartening claim: swaddling infants makes it easier to keep them asleep on their backs. Why is this important? Well, as you start to lower your newborn into the crib, you may find yourself desperately trying to remember which side the baby should sleep on to reduce the risk of SIDS. The tummy? The side? Finally, you remember: the back!

Only your baby doesn't seem to like sleeping on his back. He waves his arms around and wiggles onto his side, or startles just as he begins to fall asleep. What are you to do with this restless, fussy infant? Start with a swaddle. A snug wrap inhibits arousal, keeping baby happier on his back than if he were allowed to flail around freely, waking himself up and causing yet another round of hysteria.

Which brings us to...colic. Got colic? Studies show that colicky babies may be comforted when swaddling is combined with rocking or swinging, soothing repetitive sounds, and other types of distractions. Swaddling can lower the heart rate and keep baby calm.

To the uninitiated, swaddling looks almost cruel, like putting your sweet little darling in a straightjacket. Well, no one is suggesting that you swaddle the baby so tightly you put his hip out of joint (a rare but possible occurrence, called dysplaxia.) So how tight is just right? Wrap baby very snug, but loose enough that you can slip some fingers between baby and blankie. Proper swaddling isn't like foot binding. Yet a fairly tight wrap may still appear from your doting vantage point like facism.

Don't panic. Your baby doesn't view it this way at all. All most newborns want is to be bundled up with no chance of escape, and kept tucked by your side every minute. It's actually kind of sweet as well as scientifically sound, but alas—even science can't keep them there forever.

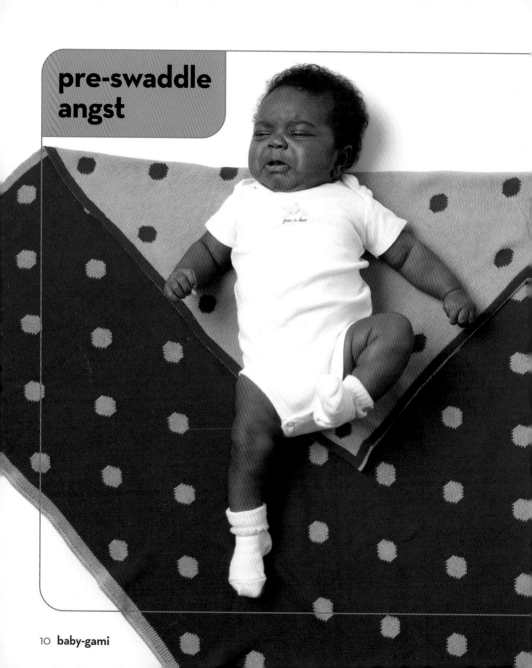

pre-swaddle
angst

post-swaddle bliss

THE REMARKABLY EFFECTIVE SWADDLE
Take one overstimulated, tired, chilly, gassy, or otherwise miserable baby, wrap her snugly in a blanket, and watch her transform . . .

. . . into a calm, relaxed (and, if you're lucky), sleepy baby.

WRAPS AND SLINGS: WHAT'S THE DIFFERENCE?

Wraps, also known as swaddles, are blankets or other pieces of fabric that you wrap snugly around baby, tucking arms and legs up close to the body. Parents have long swaddled their little ones to provide comfort, to help induce sleep, or for colic therapy. Swaddling, easily learned, can provide as much comfort to the parents as the child.

Slings are lengths of cloth that you tie securely around yourself in order to provide a pouch for baby to rest in. They're incredibly versatile: a basic cradle-style sling offers the perfect nest for a newborn, while older babies can sit happily in a sling positioned on a parent's front, side, or back. Slings offer a convenient way to "wear" your baby, and have come back into vogue after a long absence from modern infant care.

There are so many baby holders out there with modern details (belts, buckles, padded seats, DVD players) that new parents almost feel irresponsible tucking baby into a little hammock made of their own devising. Yet *Baby-gami* maintains that fancier isn't always better, for you or for baby. Try a tie or two and see how easy the slinging life can be! The following pages show a basic swaddle (page 15) and a basic sling (pages 16–17). Variations and more advanced techniques come after that.

THE BENEFITS OF BABY WRAPPING AND WEARING

Swaddling 101 is often taught by your doctor, midwife, or nurse before you're left on your own, the "burrito" wrap (page 31) being the most popular (hold the sour cream and salsa). Newborns wrapped tightly from day one tend to love their soft cocoon, yet in a few weeks they might kick their little arms and legs in resistance to being bound in such a way. DON'T assume this means it's time to kiss the wrap goodbye. That resistance has everything to do with baby's newfound strength; she might even enjoy the cozy wrap until month two or so, and with an arms-free wrap you can swaddle her for much longer. Just remember: if baby quiets down, it's working!

Wearing baby is a way to extend the gestation period: baby gets to spend an additional nine months or more in the safety and predictability of a womblike setting. New babies tucked into slings are all but invisible; parents look like they're wearing a large, saggy shoulder bag. Older babies sit high in slings, on the front, hip, or back, enjoying the ride. The serious slingophile may carry a perched rider well into the toddler years. Does it look funny to you? Think about it. Toddlers want to be carried all the time—why not get some assistance with your load? Baby's happy, and your hands are free to dial the sitter for that much-needed night out. If that's not enough to convince you to wear your baby, consider these benefits compiled by baby guru Dr. William Sears:

SLING BABIES CRY LESS: Anthropologists who study infant care have discovered that babies in baby-wearing cultures cry less frequently, and for shorter periods. And parents of fussy babies who try baby wearing often report that it cures the fussiness.

SLING BABIES LEARN MORE: If baby spends less time fussing and carrying on, then she'll spend more time in that state of calm alertness that lends itself to learning. Many slings afford baby a 180-degree opportunity to scan her surroundings. And the close proximity of mom or dad offers lots of opportunities to interact and grow.

SLING BABIES ARE MORE QUICKLY SOCIALIZED: A baby in a sling becomes intimately involved in the world of the wearer. He sees what mom and dad see, hears what they hear, learning as he goes. Facial expressions, body language, and changes in breathing and tone of voice are all experienced firsthand, as baby is carried along through the day-to-day routines of the parent.

SLING BABIES ARE SMARTER: Environmental experiences help stimulate baby's nerve endings, facilitating the growth and development of her brain. Because baby wearing brings baby out into mom and dad's environment, she gets lots of stimulation while enjoying the protection of a parental filter.

SLING BABIES ARE MORE "ORGANIZED": The rhythm of mom or dad's breathing, heartbeat, and walk help to calm and regulate baby, who is new to the world of daytime and nighttime schedules.

If enjoying the company of a smart, happy, well-adjusted baby doesn't persuade you to give it a try, think of the logistical benefits. Baby wearing makes breast-feeding much easier; when it's time for a meal, baby is already in position. And baby wearing makes other activities possible; with your hands free, you can accomplish anything from walking to the store to bring home more diapers to channel surfing while noshing on bonbons.

wrap basics

You understand the basic concept: you want to bring the little one back into a womblike environment without having to give birth all over again. You probably watched the first few times as a nurse or midwife wrapped your baby—a few quick, competent flips of the wrist and presto! A neatly wrapped, snug, content baby. What a great trick! How hard could it be? Then you tried it yourself. A few frustrating moments later, you probably watched as your messily wrapped baby popped out first an arm, then a leg, then with a wiggle, unwrapped himself entirely. Hmmm…could this be harder than it looks? Yes and no. Swaddling is a challenge at first, but once you get the hang of it, it gets easier and easier.

Part of what makes it easier, especially if you're a first-time parent, is that you grow more comfortable handling your baby. At first, those tiny newborn limbs seem so fragile that you may be too nervous to even contemplate folding them into a tightly wrapped blanket. But remember: that's what the pros do—if you looked into the nursery at a maternity ward, you would see rows of snugly swaddled, sleeping babies—and you can do it, too. It might also help to visualize how tightly packed your baby was in the womb—and what is a swaddle, after all, if not a re-creation of that warm and cozy nest?

Here's a photo sequence of a starter swaddle that you can practice on your newborn using a receiving or other baby blanket. This swaddle is perfect when you want to quickly wrap and then lay baby down on her back. Baby's own weight keeps it closed. It won't hold an energetically wriggling infant for long, but it's a quick and easy swaddle to start with. More complete instructions and step-by-step diagrams for specific wraps follow (see pages 23–65).

1 PLACE BABY ON TOP OF BLANKET, WITH HEAD JUST ABOVE THE FOLD.

2 TAKE ONE SIDE OF BLANKET AND TUCK IT SNUGLY OVER BABY'S SHOULDER THEN ACROSS AND DOWN UNDER THE OPPOSITE SIDE/BUTTOCK, LIKE FORMING HALF A V-NECKED SWEATER.

3 NOW BRING UP THE TAIL OF THE BLANKET AND TUCK SNUGLY WHERE THE **V** IS FORMED AT POINT A. PLACE BABY'S FREE ARM AT HER SIDE.

4 PULL THE OTHER SIDE OF THE BLANKET UP AND OVER BABY AND TUCK IT UNDER HER OPPOSITE SIDE, AS SHOWN.

sling basics

So you're ready to wear baby—how to get started? A piece of slightly stretchy fabric at least 5 feet (1.5 m) in length and of standard width is all you need to make a simple cross-wrap sling. This sling is a tried-and-true tradition in many cultures, and holds baby securely against your body, while distributing her weight across your back and hips so you don't end up at the chiropractor. It's versatile, too, allowing you to wear baby in front or back. More complete instructions and step-by-step diagrams for specific sling configurations follow (see pages 69–91).

1 PLACE THE CENTER OF MATERIAL ACROSS YOUR TORSO.

2 TAKE THE ENDS AND WRAP THEM BEHIND YOU, CRISSCROSSING THEM OVER YOUR SHOULDERS TO FORM AN **X** ACROSS YOUR BACK. TAILS WILL HANG BY YOUR SIDES.

3 TAKE THE TAILS AND CROSS THE FABRIC IN FRONT, FORMING ANOTHER **X**. PULL TAILS AROUND TO THE BACK AND TIE. IF THERE'S EXTRA MATERIAL, WRAP AROUND TO FRONT AGAIN AND TIE.

4 FOR A FRONT-FACING SUMO-STYLE WRAP, STICK BABY IN "POCKET" OR POUCH FIRST...

5 THEN SLIDE BABY'S LEGS (ONE AT A TIME) THROUGH THE FRONT **X**. ONCE YOU GET BABY SETTLED, YOU CAN TIGHTEN THE SLING, IF NECESSARY.

6 DONE!

POUCH VARIATION: Another easy way to get baby in place: Slide baby's legs through the X first. Then take the pouch and pull it up and over baby's tummy. Like a womb with a view!

wrapping and wearing babies around the world

To new parents looking for the happiest way to transport baby, Hug-a-Bubs and Baby Björns may seem as innovative as the iPod or flat-screen TVs. But baby swaddles and slings have been used and worn by parents around the globe for centuries. What better way to tote your infant to market, travel long distances, or bring baby out into the field while you plant and plow and harvest?

In fact, the methods we outline for wrapping and wearing your twenty-first-century baby are remarkably similar to the traditional ones. And, of course, the motivation has been the same forever: keeping baby content, cozy, and only a heartbeat away.

Parents in Korea have traditionally carried babies on their backs in slings called *podaegi* (spelled several ways, pronounced POE-DAY-GEE). This rectangular piece of quilted cotton holds baby on either the front or the back. Two long straps may be wrapped and tied over the shoulders or around the wearer's middle.

Similar to the *podaegi* is the Chinese *mei tai* (pronounced MAY-TIE), which allows parents to transport young babies in front and older babies piggy-back style. The bottom straps are worn around the waist, creating a nice cloth platform where baby sits, while the top straps are brought over the shoulders and tied to the waist strap.

In ancient Japan, mothers typically tied babies to their bodies with an *obi*, a traditional sash. Later, the *onbuhimo* (pronounced ON-BOO-HE-MO), similar to the *podaegi*, became popular. Babies were worn with their tummies against the warmth of the parent's back, which was believed to prevent indigestion.

A sling more commonly seen in the West, and the basis for many of the commercial over-the-shoulder slings, is the Mexican *rebozo* (pronounced REE-BOH-ZOH). Often made from beautiful, lightweight traditional fabrics that conform to baby's body, *rebozos* are simple to tie and use. Baby rests in a pouch formed by the folded fabric, which is tied over one shoulder. (For our version, see the Hip-Hugger Sling on page 77.)

The African *kanga* (called a "kikoy" in coastal regions and sometimes a "pagne") is a long piece of cloth that can be cleverly tied to serve as anything from a dress to a tablecloth to a head scarf to—you guessed it—a terrific baby carrier. Typically baby is worn on the back and the *kanga* is tied over one shoulder or two *kangas* are used, one tied above the breasts and the other around the hips.

The Inuit of the far north wear their babies in special parkas called *amautiks* (pronounced AH-MA-TEAK). The baby rests on the mother's back, and a voluminous hood can be pulled over both to keep them warm and cozy.

More unusual carriers include the Native American cradleboard, where baby is carried in a sort of woven backpack (used more for ceremonial and decorative purposes these days). Perhaps the most delightfully different approach to baby-gami is the New Guinea *bilium* (pronounced BILL-LEE-UM), a mesh bag Mom wears over her head with baby nestled in a pocket.

Of course, it makes perfect sense that parents around the world would have developed appropriate methods for toting their babies around—necessity being the mother of invention, and mothers, as we know, being great inventors.

Who knew there were so many ways to hold and tote a child? Now you do. So the next time you feel culturally illiterate, stop to think: whenever you put on a sling, you're on board with both a happy baby and a unifying global tradition. Peace out!

TIE ONE ON

There you have it, the basics of wrapping and slinging baby. Yet at this point we're far from ready to call it a wrap. What follows is a variety of ways to swaddle baby, and several ways to wear a sling. There are basic wraps, emergency wraps, and special occasion wraps. There are slings for cocktail parties, slings for work, slings for play.

Check it out: the permutations of baby-gami are endless!

Okay, so we're a little obsessed. But look who's talking? We know all about your pursuit of the perfect breathing coach. We know how much time it took you to pick a name. We know about the hours spent at the baby furniture store, examining diaper pad texture on high-end changing tables (despite the fact that, by the time baby number two arrives, you'll be pretty much diapering on the couch 24/7).

How do we know this? Because we're obsessed with your baby, too, with keeping her safe and content, whether she's nestled in her crib or hitting the road. We have learned through the years that the ancient art of baby-gami is the key to achieving a Zen-like state of tranquility and freedom for both of you. Plus, it's fun!

Ready to wrap? Enter the world of *Baby-gami*, and see what unfolds…

HOW TO USE THE ICONS

To make it easy to determine whether a wrap or sling is right for you and your baby, we've included icons that indicate difficulty level and age range at a glance. Since every baby (and every parent) is different, think of them as helpful guidelines rather than hard-and-fast rules.

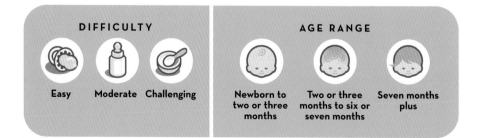

DIFFICULTY

Easy Moderate Challenging

AGE RANGE

Newborn to two or three months Two or three months to six or seven months Seven months plus

PART ONE
baby wrapping

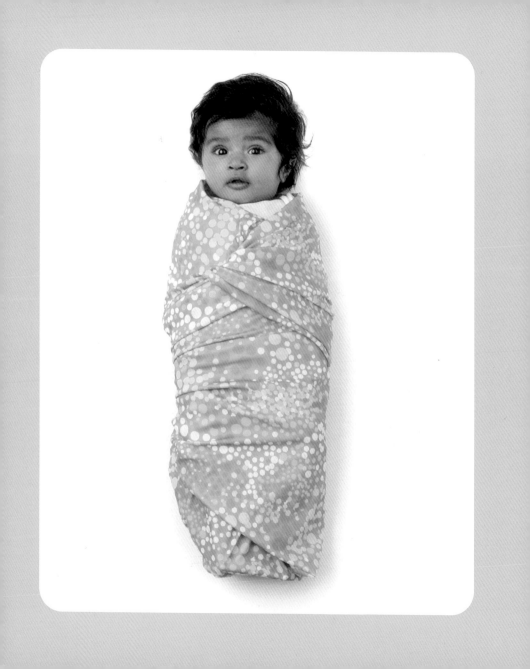

the snug wrap

When it's time to swaddle, we recommend you start with the classic Snug Wrap. Brand-new babies do best with a wrap that envelops them completely, just like your loving arms.

DIFFICULTY: Hard, at first, then moderate, then easy (just like baby herself!).

AGE RANGE: Newborn to two months (some babies enjoy it longer).

SITUATION: Always good for newborns, and for fussy or just-getting-sleepy babies.

MATERIALS: One rectangular baby blanket or piece of cloth with some stretch to the fabric. Those sweet little receiving blankets are great for baby's very first wrap or a quick swaddle. Yet to make a really good snug, you'll need a larger cloth with more give. A large crib blanket or somewhat stretchy piece of material around 2 feet by 3 feet (62 cm by 92 cm) will do the trick.

GETTING STARTED: Make sure baby's arms are straight down at her sides before you start wrapping.

1 BEGIN BY PLACING A RECTANGULAR BLANKET ON A FLAT SURFACE IN A DIAMOND SHAPE. TAKE THE TOP CORNER AND FOLD IT DOWN SO THAT THE TOP POINT IS EVEN WITH THE POINT ON THE SHORT SIDE.

2 PLACE BABY ON TOP OF BLANKET, WITH SHOULDERS JUST BELOW THE FOLD.

3 HOLDING BABY'S RIGHT ARM AT HER SIDE, GRAB THE BLANKET A FEW INCHES FROM HER RIGHT SHOULDER AND PULL IT DOWN AND ACROSS HER BODY. KEEPING THE BLANKET TAUT, TUCK IT UNDER HER LEFT BUTTOCK AND LOWER BACK. THEN, HOLDING THE BLANKET AGAINST HER LEFT HIP, GRAB THE BLANKET NEXT TO HER LEFT SHOULDER AND TUG IT DOWN TO REMOVE ANY SLACK.

5 TUCK IN THE MATERIAL AT TOP RIGHT SLIGHTLY, JUST SO IT'S OUT OF THE WAY. THEN TAKE THE RIGHT SIDE OF THE FABRIC AND BRING IT ALL THE WAY OVER, UNDER, AND BACK AROUND BABY, LIKE A BELT.

4 NOW, HOLDING HER LEFT ARM AT HER SIDE, BRING UP THE BOTTOM CORNER OF THE BLANKET AND TUCK IT SNUGLY BEHIND HER LEFT SHOULDER (IF THE MATERIAL WON'T GO QUITE THAT FAR, TUCK IT INTO THE **V** AT HER NECK).

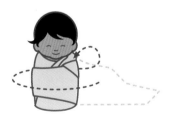

6 FINALLY, TUCK THAT LAST CORNER INTO THE **V** OF THE WRAP, AS SHOWN.

TIP

With each pull and tuck, check to see that you've wrapped baby tightly. How tight is just right? You should barely be able to slide your hand between the blanket and the baby's chest. Any looser than that and your good work will unravel before your eyes. You don't want that, and neither does your happily swaddled baby.

the fast wrap

Once your baby has had a little time to absorb the shock of life outside the womb—"Who are these giant-faced people? Why do they keep calling me 'Charlotte'? What the heck's an umbilical cord?"—she's ready for some wrap variations. The Fast Wrap is quick and secure, but not as tight as the Snug: perfect for babies who prefer a little wiggle room, and just the ticket when you are in a hurry. Once you get the hang of this one, you can practically wrap baby in your sleep (a good thing, as you'll be at least half-asleep from now on).

DIFFICULTY: Easy.

AGE RANGE: Newborn to about six months.

SITUATION: Great for warming baby up, a quick diaper cover—any time when the wrap doesn't need to last.

MATERIALS: Receiving blanket for newborns, baby blanket for older ones.

basic wraps 27

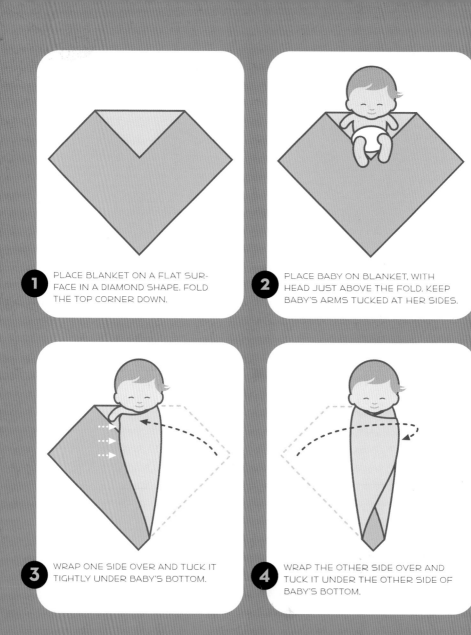

1 PLACE BLANKET ON A FLAT SUR-
FACE IN A DIAMOND SHAPE. FOLD
THE TOP CORNER DOWN.

2 PLACE BABY ON BLANKET, WITH
HEAD JUST ABOVE THE FOLD. KEEP
BABY'S ARMS TUCKED AT HER SIDES.

3 WRAP ONE SIDE OVER AND TUCK IT
TIGHTLY UNDER BABY'S BOTTOM.

4 WRAP THE OTHER SIDE OVER AND
TUCK IT UNDER THE OTHER SIDE OF
BABY'S BOTTOM.

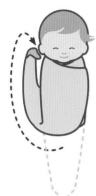

5 BRING THE TAIL UP, UNDER BABY'S FEET AND BEHIND HER BACK, AND TUCK IT INTO THE FOLD TO SECURE IT.

6 ALL TUCKED IN!

When nursing, sometimes it's easier for both of you if the wrap lands a bit lower on baby's shoulders. Experiment for your perfect fit.

TIP

the burrito wrap

The Burrito Wrap is the standard-issue wrap. More secure than the Fast Wrap, it's a bit trickier to execute but still pretty easy, providing your little one isn't strenuously trying to wiggle his way out. Baby has plenty of freedom from the neck up, while the body is tucked in tight.

DIFFICULTY: Moderate but may be a bit challenging the first time.

AGE RANGE: Newborn to about six months.

SITUATION: Your best option when baby decides the Snug Wrap is too snug.

MATERIALS: One baby blanket with some stretch • One pitcher of margaritas to go with your burrito. (Just kidding. Never drink and wrap.)

a wrap by any other name

Not a burrito fan? Feel free to rename baby's favorite wrap after any of these other fine cuisine coverings:

CHINESE	**Egg Roll**
INDIAN	**Samosa**
FRENCH	**Crêpe**
MIDWESTERN	**Pig-in-a-Blanket**

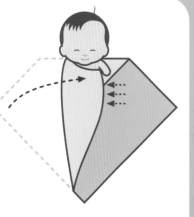

1 AS FOR THE FAST WRAP (PAGE 27), ARRANGE THE BLANKET IN A DIAMOND SHAPE WITH THE TOP CORNER FOLDED DOWN. PLACE BABY ON BLANKET WITH HEAD JUST ABOVE THE FOLD, THEN WRAP ONE SIDE OVER AND TUCK IT UNDER BABY'S BOTTOM.

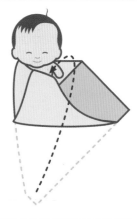

2 NEXT, BRING THE BOTTOM CORNER UP AND TUCK IT IN, NEAR BABY'S NECK.

3 FOLD THE OTHER SIDE OVER AND TUCK IT BEHIND BABY'S SHOULDER TO FORM A V-NECK.

4 THE FINISHED WRAP.

wrap you up in my love:

HOMEMADE WRAP HOW-TOS

Maternity fashions may have entered the new millennium, but pastels and teddy bears still dominate clothing and accessories in the infant aisles. Sure baby looks great in everything, but why limit her? Bust out of the nursery clichés and make your own blanket for baby! It may sound like a tall order if you're sleep deprived (not to mention craft impaired), but if you have time for a quick trip to the fabric store, you can whip up a cozy little wrap. Difficulty ranges from super-simple to pretty darn easy.

THE SUPER-SIMPLE WRAP (USE PINKING SHEARS)

1) Go to the fabric store. Pass by the overly precious pastels and make a beeline for a pattern or color you love. (The fabric should be stretchy and breathable.) Buy a yard (about 1 meter) in a 52-inch width (1⅓ meters).
2) Trim around the edges with pinking shears to create a decorative finish and keep blanket from fraying. That's it!

THE SIMPLE WRAP (USE FUSIBLE HEMMING)

1) Follow step 1 above. In addition, buy some fusible hemming material at the fabric store.
2) Now heat up your trusty iron. Create a quick hem by folding over the edges of the material and ironing on the fusible hemming.

THE PRETTY-SIMPLE WRAP (SEWING MACHINE REQUIRED)

1) Follow step 1 for the Super-Simple Wrap.
2) You know how to sew? Then you don't need us to tell you what to do next. Go ahead and hem the fabric using your favorite stitch. Instant baby wrap!

the after-bath cuddle wrap

Whether your baby views bath time as a visit to the spa or a scene from *Jaws*, he will no doubt appreciate a post-bath wrap in a wonderfully fluffy towel made just for drying babies. This wrap is a loose variation on the Fast Wrap—it's quick (after all, you don't want baby getting chilled) and it doesn't have to last.

DIFFICULTY: Moderate. (Warning: babies are slippery when wet.)

AGE RANGE: For all ages.

SITUATION: Rub-a-dub-dub.

MATERIALS: One baby bath towel with hood • Rubber ducky (optional).

GETTING STARTED: Before you lift baby up and out of his bath, be ready with a nice hooded towel.

NOTE: We know that you know NEVER to leave baby in the bath alone, for even a second. It's pretty obvious when he's this tiny. Yet you'd be amazed how many parents think that once baby can sit up confidently, he can be abandoned for a quick phone call or trip to the other bathroom for more baby shampoo. Wrong, wrong, wrong. Picture your baby as essentially welded to your arm during bathing—you'll never be sorry.

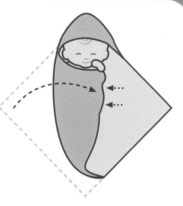

1 PLACE THE HOOD ON BABY'S HEAD, AND WRAP THE TOWEL LOOSELY AROUND BABY'S SHOULDERS.

2 LAY BABY DOWN AND WRAP ONE SIDE OVER AND TUCK IT LOOSELY UNDER BABY'S BOTTOM. WRAP THE OTHER SIDE OVER, BUT LEAVE THE END UNTUCKED.

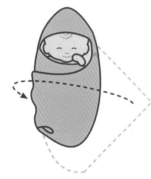

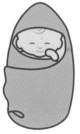

3 USE END OF TOWEL TO GENTLY YET QUICKLY PAT BABY DRY ALL OVER. DON'T NEGLECT THOSE HARD-TO-REACH CREASES IN BABY'S SKIN.

4 CONTINUE TO PAT BABY DRY. BUT DON'T DAWDLE: GET THAT DIAPER ON OR YOU MIGHT HAVE TO REPEAT THE BATH! (SQUEAKY RUBBER DUCKY CAN BE USED TO DISTRACT BABY AS YOU DRY HIM.)

what NOT to use for swaddling baby

Every parent has been there: tired, stressed out, yearning for baby to sleep—or at least stop wailing. Yet in our passionate pursuit of peace, we can unintentionally cause true harm by wrapping baby in something ill-suited for that purpose. Avoid these swaddling dangers:

DON'T USE	WHY
Angora	Tickles nose, gets in baby's mouth
Cashmere	No match for spit-up
Wool	Too scratchy
Fabric with buttons or snaps	Baby may pop them off and swallow them
Fabric with zippers	Pinched skin
Newspaper	Unsafe inks, disturbing editorials
Silky fabrics	Too slippery
Chiffon	Not warm enough
Retro-image print	Baby can't appreciate irony
Day-Glo colored fabric	Not restful
Animal print	Menacing to family pet (exception: for Halloween)
Plaid	Ugly

the arms-free wrap

Congratulations! You have raised baby to the point where she actually looks comfortable out of the womb. Maybe she's not quite ready to help carry in the groceries, but those little arms love to move around. Try this comfy wrap for the baby who can no longer keep her hands to herself.

DIFFICULTY: Easy.

AGE RANGE: Two months on.

SITUATION: For Burrito-Wrap-resistant babies.

MATERIALS: One receiving blanket.

NOTE: This is like the Fast Wrap (page 27) only it just covers the bottom half.

basic wraps 39

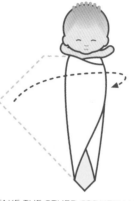

1. FOLD DOWN TOP OF BLANKET, PLACE BABY WITH HER WAIST AT TOP OF FOLD. TAKE ONE CORNER AND PULL IT TIGHT ACROSS BABY'S BODY. LIFT BABY'S OPPOSITE SIDE UP AND TUCK WRAP SNUGLY UNDER HER BACK .

2. TAKE THE OTHER CORNER AND BRING IT ACROSS TO THE OTHER SIDE, TUCKING IT SNUGLY UNDER HER BACK, AS SHOWN.

3. BRING TAIL UP BEHIND BABY AND TUCK IT IN.

4. THERE YOU HAVE IT—THE ARMS ARE FREE TO EXPLORE, BUT BABY IS STILL COZILY TUCKED IN!

how to soothe baby

In the beginning, your choices were simple: feed baby, rock baby, cuddle baby. One of those tried-and-true methods usually did the trick. Yet when baby starts to bust out of his tightest wraps, he'll need a little variety in the soothing department. Here's a quick checklist of dependable methods to chill out a frazzled baby, in or out of a wrap.

GET MOVING: Of course, putting baby in a sling or in your arms and dancing, walking, or rocking is always the first method to try. Going outside, where he can experience strange sounds and new temperatures, is often a curative for baby's inner pandemonium. Sometimes a drive is in order; for babies who love the car, a few blocks is often all it takes to help them transition into blissful sleep.

GET VISUAL: Ceiling fans rival pets, other children, and television when it comes to enthralling distractions for baby, who's always eager to take in new sights with plenty of movement. Look around your house for anything else (or anyone) that might provide a show.

GET NOISY: You may hate the vacuum cleaner, or wish you had a quieter dishwasher. Yet white noise is often a panacea to the bewildered baby. If you discover a sound that works like magic, make a tape to play anytime baby needs soothing, whether or not you have dirty carpets or dishes.

GET WOMBLIKE: If stimulation just makes baby cry harder, he might be homesick for that early "rental." Try a bottle or pacifier, a tight wrap or sling, a comforting cuddle in a dark, quiet room—anything that shuts out the big free-for-all world that has replaced his first home. The best part about this approach? It might just chill you out, too.

the kitchen-towel wrap

The rest of the house is asleep, and since baby is feeling lively despite the late hour, you've brought him downstairs to help you forage for a midnight snack. Yet just as you tuck into your ham and pickle sandwich, he grows restless, and soon his fretful murmurs will turn into a shriek. What to do? If your kitchen is equipped with a couple of clean towels, he'll be at peace—and you'll be enjoying a well-deserved nosh—in no time. Also good during daytime food prep…

DIFFICULTY: Moderate (depending on how tired and hungry you are).

AGE RANGE: Newborn to about two months.

SITUATION: For kitchen prowling and cooking.

MATERIALS: Two freshly laundered kitchen towels.

NOTE: Even clean kitchen towels don't belong right on baby's tender skin. Make sure he's got a onesie or night clothes on under the wrap.

1 LAY A KITCHEN TOWEL DOWN ON A CLEAN, DRY SURFACE. PLACE ANOTHER ONE OVER IT, OVERLAPPING ALL BUT 6 OR 7 INCHES (15 TO 18 CM) ON THE LEFT.

2 GENTLY TURN THE TOWELS TO THE RIGHT UNTIL THEY LAY IN A DIAMOND SHAPE. FOLD OVER TOP CORNERS TOGETHER, AS SHOWN.

3 PLACE BABY ON TOWELS WITH CHEST JUST BELOW TOP, ARMS FREE, SLIGHTLY TO ONE SIDE OF CENTER. WRAP ONE SIDE OVER AND TUCK IT TIGHTLY UNDER BABY'S BOTTOM.

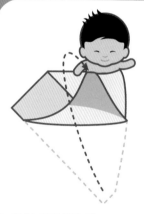

4 PULL THE TAIL UP AND TUCK INTO V-NECK.

5 PULL THE OTHER SIDE UP AND ACROSS CHEST, AND TUCK IN BABY.

6 YOU'RE DONE! BABY IS BUNDLED AND EASY TO HOLD WHILE YOU CHOMP INTO THAT HEALTHY SNACK.

TIP

You can usually burp a small baby while he's swaddled, but if relief does not come quickly, freeing his arms might help. An older baby will need to be unwrapped for burping, but be sure to tuck him back in when you're done. A snug swaddle after a good meal is likely to send him straight to the Land of Nod.

the paper-bag wrap

It happens. Baby has an explosion (from one end or the other!), the outfit is ruined, and to your horror you realize that the spare you meant to put in the diaper bag is back at home. Or you've gone through two outfits already. You need a quick cover for baby until you can get him home. Voilà! A paper bag will do the trick, protecting baby from the environment (and vice versa) until real clothes can be found. (You'll notice that a sack of groceries may weigh more than a sack of baby, but it doesn't squirm as much.)

DIFFICULTY: Easy.

AGE RANGE: Two months to one year.

SITUATION: For desperate times!

MATERIALS: One empty, reasonably clean paper bag.

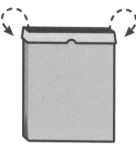

1 OPEN OUT BAG FULLY, THEN FOLD OVER THE TOP EDGE (TO AVOID ROUGH SPOTS FROM TOUCHING BABY'S SKIN).

2 SLIP BABY INTO BAG.

3 MAKE CREASE USING EXTRA PAPER IN THE CENTER OF BAG.

4 FOLD OVER SMALL PIECE AT TOP OF CREASE ON RIGHT SIDE.

5 TUCK EDGE OVER FOLDED EDGE TO "LOCK" BAG IN PLACE.

6 IT'S IN THE BAG! (NOTE: THIS WRAP WON'T HOLD FOR LONG. BUT IT'LL DO IN A PINCH.)

If your wrap unravels, don't make the novice's mistake of thinking you can rewrap a sleeping baby without waking him up. Scratch that plan. What is there to do but gaze at your unwrapped miracle, the darling spindliness of his legs, the way his tufts of hair waft in the breeze, the curve of his sweet, plump cheek? Moments later, when baby wakes up screaming like a banshee, put that wrap back in place.

TIP

the map wrap

With baby on board, you're ready for a show-and-tell car trip. Yet how do you keep the peace with this high-maintenance passenger? You stop to feed baby, you stop to change baby—sometimes you pull over just because he's miserable. Left his favorite blankie at home? Wrap baby up in a large paper map for quick comfort. With a Map Wrap, he'll always know where he's at…

DIFFICULTY: Moderate (depending on state of map, and fussiness of baby).

AGE RANGE: Newborn to about three months.

SITUATION: On the Road Again.

MATERIALS: One large, clean, paper map. (You can always buy one at the gas station, or if you're taking public transportation, pick up a free map when you buy your ticket.)

NOTE: This wrap is similar to the Fast Wrap (page 27); the difference is in the first few folds.

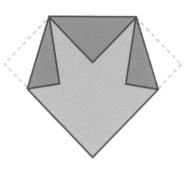

1 PLACE THE MAP ON A FLAT SURFACE AND FOLD DOWN THE TOP CORNER. TAKE EACH SIDE OF THE MAP AND FOLD DOWN A SEGMENT, AS SHOWN.

2 IF EDGES SEEM SHARP, SOFTEN THEM BY CRINKLING THE PAPER SLIGHTLY.

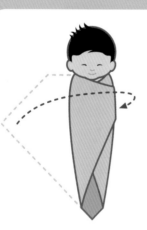

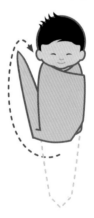

3 WRAP ONE SIDE OVER AND TUCK IT TIGHTLY UNDER BABY'S BOTTOM. REPEAT WITH THE OTHER SIDE.

4 BRING THE TAIL UP BEHIND BABY AND TUCK INTO THE BACK FOLD TO SECURE.

road trip blues:

HOW TO CALM BABY WHILE ON THE MOVE

 There's scarcely a parent out there who hasn't experienced Travel Hysteria (except for those poor souls whose colicky children are only calm while riding in a car). Your tiny traveler doesn't know that you can't just stop the car (bus, plane, train, or boat) and let him off, so here are some parent-tested, parent-approved distractions.

PEEK-A-BOO is often a winner. Even if baby is too young to understand that you're hiding, she might pause in her tirade to wonder why you no longer have a face. Another good trick: pull out a small mirror and hold it up to baby. The wonder of seeing another baby—right in her very own car!—may settle her down pronto.

SING, SING, AND SING SOME MORE. Who cares if you have a terrible voice? It can't be any worse than baby's car-alarm imitation. "Twinkle, Twinkle Little Star" works well, as does "The Itsy-Bitsy Spider," a tale of courage and perseverance with arresting hand motions. However, in this situation, enthusiasm matters far more than age appropriateness. Feel free to belt out that old Nirvana tune.

BRIBERY IS A TRIED-AND-TRUE TECHNIQUE. Try slipping baby a pacifier, a bottle, or a new toy. For older babies, a bottle, some juice, or a treat (yes, that means sugar) may stem the tide long enough for you to reach your destination.

Can't calm baby and there are miles yet to go? If you're in your own car, crank the radio and let him cry it out—or pull over until the storm subsides. If you're on public transportation, ignore the glares from your fellow passengers, take a deep breath, and try your arsenal of tricks again.

the diaper-changing wrap

Changing baby in an airport lounge or on a car seat is no walk in the park. Add in a tiny pair of flailing arms and you've really got your work cut out for you. Both parent and baby will be much happier if those movable parts are contained in a nice, snug wrap while you do your "dirty work."

DIFFICULTY: Moderate (depending on messiness of baby).

AGE RANGE: Newborn to six months (or longer, if you face a true emergency).

SITUATION: Quick-Change Stop.

MATERIALS: One baby blanket, wipes and diaper at the ready.

NOTE: This wrap might also prove useful during your son's bris.

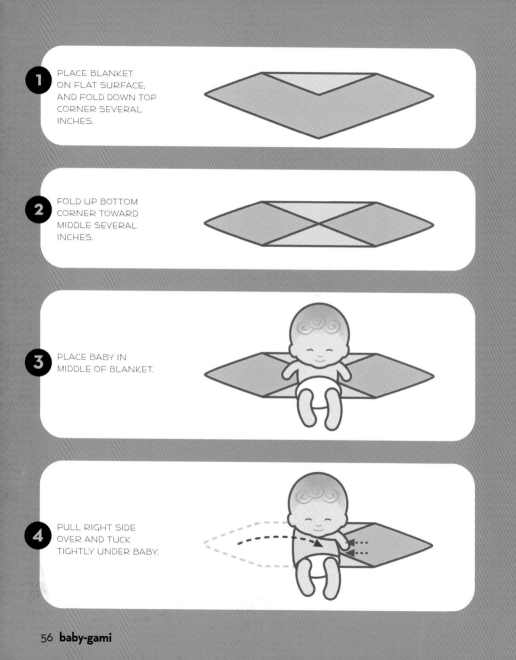

1 PLACE BLANKET ON FLAT SURFACE, AND FOLD DOWN TOP CORNER SEVERAL INCHES.

2 FOLD UP BOTTOM CORNER TOWARD MIDDLE SEVERAL INCHES.

3 PLACE BABY IN MIDDLE OF BLANKET.

4 PULL RIGHT SIDE OVER AND TUCK TIGHTLY UNDER BABY.

5 WRAP LEFT SIDE OVER AND UNDER BABY, THEN TUCK THE END TIGHTLY INTO FOLD IN BACK.

6 NOW CHANGE THAT DIAPER: QUICKLY!

changing tips

Be sure to have everything you need—fresh diapers, wipes or cotton balls, and ointment—right at hand. Newborns are better off without fancy scented wipes; a simple wipe, cotton pad, or cloth doused in lukewarm water is best for sensitive skin.

Wipe thoroughly, yet don't be so studious in your efforts that baby lets out an impatient howl every time you set her on the table. With girls, be sure to clean all the crevices, but don't pull back the lips of the vulva.

Slide a fresh diaper under baby's bottom, then apply petroleum jelly, or if baby has a rash, medicated diaper ointment (the usual active ingredient is zinc oxide). Do up the diaper snugly but with a finger of room so baby's tummy can expand as needed. With boys, before rediapering, be careful to tuck the penis in so it points downward to prevent leaks.

the gift wrap

Whether it's Grandma's birthday or one of the winter gift-giving extravaganzas, what present could be more welcome than everyone's favorite baby wrapped up like the best gift ever? No receipt needed.

DIFFICULTY: Easy.

AGE RANGE: Newborn to about six months.

MATERIALS: Satin material, the size of a baby blanket • About 3 feet (92 cm) of tulle.

DIRECTIONS:

1. Do a Fast Wrap (pages 28–29) and tuck in back.
2. Place tulle behind baby, and tie in an enclosing but gentle bow.

NOTE: Remember, the bows are just for fun during the gift-opening portion of the event. Take a picture, then unwrap her! Never put baby in the crib with ribbons of any sort. (In addition to the obvious choking or strangling hazards, she might attempt to tie them into a rope in order to escape the family's hideously off-key holiday singing.)

special occasion wraps   59

the picnic wrap

Chasing winter away with baby's first picnic? She'll look as fresh as spring in this festive "edible" wrap. Plus, you can use her to hold down one end of the picnic blanket.

DIFFICULTY: Easy.

AGE RANGE: Newborn to about six months.

MATERIALS: One sunny day • One square of soft, picnic-inspired cotton or other breathable fabric.

DIRECTIONS: Either the Burrito (page 32) or Fast Wrap (pages 28-29) will work nicely for this outdoor adventure wrap.

NOTE: We know that you know that baby should get NO harmful UV rays on her newborn skin. Top off this fetching wrap with a smart sun hat and make sure baby stays in the shade. Diligent parents often check children for reddening skin, but you usually can't see a sunburn until after it's developed—too late for the miserable baby, whose thin skin makes her particularly at risk. Babies under six months can't wear sunscreen and their time under the rays should be limited. Older babies need a ton of SPF (we recommend 30 or higher) and should also be protected with hats, shirts, and plenty of shade.

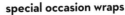

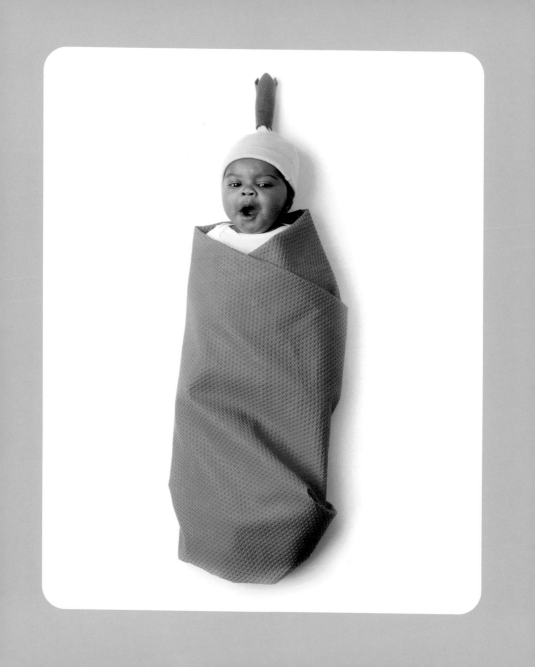

the halloween wrap

The moon is full, the candy is in the bowl...it's your first Halloween as a parent! Sort of sorry you didn't whip up a creative costume for your little pumpkin? Well, guess what? A little pumpkin she can be, thanks to a few yards of fabric and your new-found wrapping expertise.

DIFFICULTY: Moderate (if you include hat).

AGE RANGE: Newborn to about six months.

MATERIALS: One pumpkin-colored cloth, crib-blanket size • One bright green infant hat, preferably topped with a nubbin or pompom • 6 inches (15 cm) green felt • Glue, hot glue, or other strong sealant • Needle and green thread • Scissors.

DIRECTIONS:

1. For the Body: Use a Fast Wrap (pages 28–29) with a back tuck.

2. For the Hat: Cut felt into a zigzag on one end. Glue long ends together to form a tube. Slide tube over hat nubbin, pompom, or whatever decorative bauble the hat has on top. (You can add a few stitches for extra security.)

3. Happy Halloween! Your baby looks the part, whether bright-eyed under the moonlight or asleep in the pumpkin patch.

the winter wrap

Before baby, you might have been shy about popping into lobbies and stores when a sudden fierce wind picked up. Now that you have to stay warm for two, banish that bashfulness. Just pick a noisy coffee shop over a quiet-as-death boutique and no one will mind that you're only shopping for better weather. While you wait, this fleecy wrap will keep baby cozy.

DIFFICULTY: Easy; baby will enjoy this snuggly wrap.

AGE RANGE: Newborn to about three months (or longer, if it's really nippy outside).

MATERIALS: One fleece baby's blanket. An adjustable stroller (one that lies flat) can also come in handy here.

DIRECTIONS: Follow instructions for the Snug Wrap (pages 24–25).

special occasion wraps

sleep, baby, sleep

We love wraps because they're cute, they're warm, and they're womblike. Most of all, we love them because, along with nursing and baths, rubbing and rocking, they help us get baby to sleep. A soothing lullaby is the finishing touch that seals the deal. Below are some of the classics that have helped generations of babies slide gently into dreamland. (If you've forgotten the lyrics, visit www.babycenter.com/baby/babysleep/index, or just hum the tune. Baby won't mind.)

All the Pretty Horses

All Through the Night

Amazing Grace

Clementine

Day Is Done

Frere Jacques
  (Are You Sleeping?)

Golden Slumbers

Hush, Little Baby

Itsy-Bitsy Spider

Lavender's Blue
  (Dilly Dilly)

Lullaby and Good Night
  (Brahm's Lullaby)

Rock-a-Bye Baby

Sleep, Baby, Sleep

Swing Low, Sweet Chariot

Toora Loora, Loora

PART TWO
baby wearing

BASIC SLINGS

the front sling

It's hard for new parents to believe that a simple piece of cloth can hold baby as safely and happily as all the expensive baby-carrying contraptions on the market—but it can! Worn like a favorite old shirt, the Front Sling provides baby with a comfy perch and frees you up to do a multitude of things. It works best if baby can hold her head up and loves to look out at the world. She can also face toward you—a great position for nursing.

This sling is the basic cross-wrap version (for step-by-step photos, see pages 16–17). We find it to be the easiest and most comfortable of the many tie-on sling variations. The baby's weight is distributed across your torso, so you can tote around your 18-pound bundle without strain.

DIFFICULTY: Moderate (until you get the hang of it).

AGE RANGE: Once baby can hold her head up to until she (or you) tire of it.

MATERIALS: 2 to 3 yards (184 cm to 276 cm) of breathable fabric in standard width. It should have some degree of "give" but not be super stretchy.

1 PLACE THE CENTER PORTION OF THE MATERIAL LENGTHWISE ACROSS YOUR TORSO.

2 TAKE THE ENDS AND WRAP THEM BEHIND YOU, CRISSCROSSING THEM OVER YOUR SHOULDERS. THE FABRIC SHOULD FORM AN **X** ACROSS YOUR BACK AS SHOWN.

3 TAKE THE ENDS HANGING DOWN BY YOUR SIDES AND CROSS THE FABRIC IN FRONT. NOW PULL THE TAILS AROUND TO THE BACK AND TIE.

4 IF THERE'S EXTRA MATERIAL, WRAP THE CLOTH BACK AROUND TO THE FRONT AND TIE.

5 YOU'LL SEE A POUCH CREATED BY THE MATERIAL IN FRONT. STICK BABY IN POUCH.

6 IF BABY'S LEGS ARE LONG ENOUGH, LOOP CRISSCROSS UNDER LEGS, AS SHOWN. IF NOT, CRISSCROSS UNDER BABY'S TUCKED-IN FEET.

Some sling instruc-tions suggest putting baby in before you're all tied up. We recommend finishing the sling and then sliding in baby. You can always tighten the tie after she's placed in her carrier for the perfect fit.

TIP

the back sling

Don't fear the Back Sling, even though it sounds like the name of an off-hand insult to your parenting: "Is the baby going outside dressed like that?" his aunt back-slinged. The Back Sling frees you to do things that you don't want baby participating in (such as cooking or applying mascara). Older babies love it too. Someday he'll cry, "Piggy back ride!" on his own. For now, just assume he'd love to try this fun and comfy sling ride.

DIFFICULTY: Moderate.

AGE RANGE: Once baby can hold his head up to as long as you both enjoy it.

MATERIALS: 2 to 3 yards (184 cm to 276 cm) of breathable fabric in standard width. It should have some degree of "give" but not be super stretchy.

NOTE: This is just like the Front Sling (page 69), only reversed. Loading the back sling looks like a two-parent operation, yet experienced slingers can bend over and put (older) babies in by themselves. Why not work up to that?

basic slings 73

1 PLACE MIDDLE SECTION OF FABRIC ACROSS YOUR MIDDLE BACK, NEAR YOUR WAIST-LINE. (THIS WILL FORM A POUCH.)

2 CROSS ENDS IN FRONT, FORMING AN **X**.

3 BRINGS ENDS OVER YOUR SHOULDERS TO THE BACK. CROSS IN BACK, AS SHOWN.

4 BRING ENDS AROUND TO THE FRONT. TIE IN FRONT.

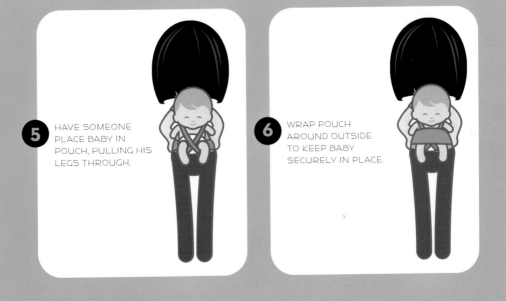

5 HAVE SOMEONE PLACE BABY IN POUCH, PULLING HIS LEGS THROUGH.

6 WRAP POUCH AROUND OUTSIDE TO KEEP BABY SECURELY IN PLACE.

TIP

If your back begins to feel strained while wearing a sling, make sure your baby is positioned above your waist and pulled close to your body. Tighten and adjust the sling accordingly. You may need to experiment a little to find a fit that works for both baby and you.

the hip-hugger sling

This is the easiest sling of all! Based on the Mexican *rebozo*, it is a simple over-the-shoulder tie that works for any baby, from newborn to toddler. For newborns, the fabric creates a "cradle" in which baby can lie snugly nestled against your chest. For older babies, the fabric creates a pocket in which baby can sit up, securely astride mom or dad's hip, and take in the view.

DIFFICULTY: Easy.

AGE RANGE: Newborn to as long as you both enjoy it.

SITUATION: A quick sling for a busy life.

MATERIALS: 3 to 6 feet (1 to 2 meters) fabric of standard width (cotton is nice).

1 FOLD FABRIC IN HALF LENGTHWISE. PUT IT OVER YOUR SHOULDER DIAGONALLY, ENDS AT OPPOSITE HIP TO DRAPED SHOULDER. TIE ENDS IN A DOUBLE KNOT.

2 SLIDE KNOT UP AND OVER YOUR SHOULDER. PULL EDGE OF CLOTH ON SHOULDER OVER SO IT'S A BIT DOWN ON YOUR ARM.

3 THE FABRIC CREATES A POUCH. PLACE TINY BABIES INSIDE LIKE A CRADLE, FOR OLDER ONES, SLIDE LEGS IN FIRST, SETTLE BABY'S BOTTOM IN POUCH, AS SHOWN.

4 CHECK TO SEE BABY IS SNUG IN POUCH, WITH WALL OF FABRIC SURROUNDING HIM, AND YOU'RE DONE!

baby wearing guidelines

The benefits of wearing a sling are worth the brief period it takes to master the technique. The following tips will help:

1) **WEAR YOUR SLING AS SNUGLY AS IS COMFORTABLE FOR YOU AND BABY.** Yet don't assume you're doing something wrong if sling wearing feels precarious at first. Get a good, tight fit and then hold the sling in the crook of your arm until you feel comfortable with the balance of weight.

2) **DON'T WEAR A FRONT OR BACK SLING BELOW THE WAIST;** that's too tough on your back. Other than that rule, experiment with positions and styles. The best way to wear baby is what's best for the two of you.

3) **GIVE YOUR BODY TIME TO ADJUST TO THE ADDED WEIGHT OF YOUR SLING.** Although sling wearing is an excellent way to strengthen your muscles, just like with any other kind of workout, you need to start slowly, gradually building your endurance. Try no more than half an hour at first.

the glamour sling

Can't find a sitter? Never fear: bring baby along for a night on the town. A sling is the perfect accessory, especially a hip-hugger, which can be worn just like a shoulder bag.

Choose a fabric that suits your occasion. Animal prints and shiny silks say casual elegance, while for a black-tie ball you might want this stretchy sequined look. The only thing more dazzling than your sling will be the child inside, who looks fabulous in whatever you happen to throw on her. Remember: you may be a mother now, but you're also a woman of style who can wear a sling that says, "I may have a tot, but I still can look hot!"

POSITION: The Hip-Hugger Sling (page 77).

DIFFICULTY: Easy.

AGE RANGE: Newborn until baby insists on swiping every canapé you bring to your lips.

MATERIALS: 3 to 6 feet (1 to 2 meters) of something slinky.

WARNING: Take the child-safe fabric test: if sequins or other embellishments can be plucked off the cloth, opt for a fabric with no extras—perhaps something shimmery or velvety instead.

the office sling

The sitter is sick or the day care center is closed, but work is still on the schedule. What to do? Baby will fit right into any corporate environment in this handsome, pin-striped back sling. Even if casual dress has made its way into your company, your colleagues will appreciate your nod to classic work attire, and your infant will look polished and professional.

POSITION: You can use either a Front Sling (page 69) or a Back Sling, pictured (page 73).

DIFFICULTY: Moderate (just like you, baby may tire of ceaseless e-mailing and endless meetings).

AGE RANGE: As soon as baby can hold her head up until she gets too heavy.

MATERIALS: 2 to 3 yards (184 cm to 276 cm) of breathable fabric in standard width. Choose pin-stripes or another office-appropriate fabric.

WARNING: If baby can't resist helping you type, back slings are best.

"your ad here" sling

Everyone loves to look at an adorable baby—so why waste good ad space? Admirers can learn about your business or unique professional services as they coo over baby, and baby can finally start to earn his keep. Some might find using a baby as an advertising venue tasteless, even exploitative. We say nonsense—why shouldn't baby contribute to the household income if he can? Got an up-and-coming business or a delightful shop? Let your new little town cryer tell us all about it.

POSITION: Use a Front Sling (page 69). That way, your ad will be the first thing everyone sees.

DIFFICULTY: Moderate.

AGE RANGE: As soon as the baby can hold his head up until you can afford to advertise in more orthodox places.

MATERIALS: 2 to 3 yards (184 cm to 276 cm) of breathable fabric in standard width. Use stick-on letters from the craft store or fusible felt ones for a more permanent ad.

the french sling

Need some fresh herbs, a fish for this evening's meal, or perhaps a baguette? Don a French Sling, inspired by shoppers in the markets of Paris. Stroll through the market and squeeze the produce with abandon while baby enjoys the view from a back sling in which the pocket can also hold some of your stuff. Très chic and convenient too. The only risk is that a hungry toddler may be tempted to eat his dinner before you get it home or otherwise play with your purchases—so be careful what you store in the sling pouch!

POSITION: The Back Sling (page 73).

DIFFICULTY: Moderate (sharing the sling with groceries may prove to be a distraction for baby).

AGE RANGE: As soon as the baby can hold his head up until he prefers to go shopping in a stroller.

MATERIALS: 2 to 3 yards (184 cm to 276 cm) of striped fabric in standard width. It should have some give but not be super stretchy.

the housework sling

"Look Dad, no hands!" The Housework Sling enables Pop to do the dishes, sweep the floors, or watch the game in peace while baby goes along for the ride. The simple domestic fabric shown is only one option; the Housework Sling works just as well in a manly flannel or a team-inspired print.

Juggling kids and house maintenance is no job for wimps. Wrapped up and ready to go, you and your little one can enjoy the important things in life: a clean house, a well-cooked meal, hours of mindless Internet surfing, or watching a sporting event just because it's on the tube. Ah, the good life!

POSITION: The Front Sling (page 69).

DIFFICULTY: Moderate.

AGE RANGE: As soon as the baby can hold his head up until you both tire of it.

MATERIALS: 2 to 3 yards (184 cm to 276 cm) of breathable fabric. Choose something that can stand up to a little dust or soap suds.

twice-the-fun sling

What's a busy parent of twins to do? Yes, the answer is to wear them both at once with this double Hip-Hugger Sling. It's easy—just follow the directions for the single Hip-Hugger—twice! Then load them up, one to a side. With a baby on each hip, you're like a cowboy from the Old West, slinging cuteness instead of guns. A word of advice: don't plan any long walks dressed in a pair of babies, as your cute burden may grow heavy rather quickly—but for a quick foray, say to the corner store for milk—this is a super solution.

POSITION: The Hip-Hugger Sling (page 77).

DIFFICULTY: Slings are easy to tie but you might need some help loading the babies.

AGE RANGE: Newborns until twice-the-fun becomes a back strain for you.

MATERIALS: Two pieces of color-coordinated fabric, 3 to 6 feet (1 to 2 meters).

special slings

meet the babies

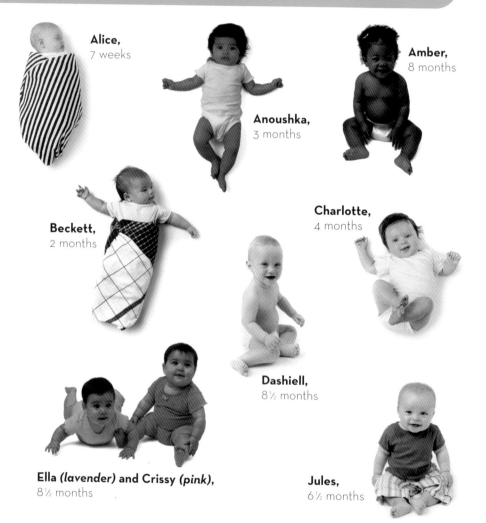

Alice,
7 weeks

Anoushka,
3 months

Amber,
8 months

Beckett,
2 months

Charlotte,
4 months

Dashiell,
8½ months

Ella (*lavender*) and Crissy (*pink*),
8½ months

Jules,
6½ months

Lizzie,
10 months

Madison,
2 months

Matthew,
11 months

Nathan,
4 months

Oliver,
11 months

Natalia,
6 months

Roan,
8 weeks

Sabrina,
4 months

Samuel,
1 year

meet the babies 93

INDEX

FOR FURTHER INFORMATION

Bernhard, Emery, and Durga, *A Ride on Mother's Back: A Day of Baby Carrying Around the World.* New York: Harcourt Brace & Co., 1996.

Borgenicht, Louis, M.D., and Joe Borgenicht, *The Baby Owner's Manual.* Philadelphia: Quirk Books, 2003.

Gerard, Harris, and Thach, *Spontaneous Arousals in Supine Infants While Swaddled and Unswaddled During Rapid Eye Movement and Quiet Sleep,* Washington University School of Medicine, St. Louis, Missouri: *Journal of Pediatrics,* September, 2003.

Karp, Harvey, M.D., *The Happiest Baby on the Block.* New York: Bantam, 2003.

Sears, William, M.D., and Martha Sears, R.N., *The Baby Book.* Boston: Little Brown, 2003.

For those interested in learning more about traditional baby carrying or purchasing all manner of wraps and slings, the Internet is a great resource. Check it out!

PHOTO CREDITS

Our thanks to the Burlington Coat Factory, Gymboree, and Planet Kids for the delightful fabrics shown in the photographs, and to WearstheBaby.com for permission to photograph their Sweet Pea Wrap, the traditional wrap carrier pictured on page 72.